Learning Is Fun!

KATHY ROSS C·R·A·F·T·S
LETTER SHAPES

by Kathy Ross
Illustrated by Jan Barger

The Millbrook Press
Brookfield, Connecticut

For Betsy, who learned these letters with me!
K.R.

Library of Congress Cataloging-in-Publication Data

Ross, Kathy (Katharine Reynolds), 1948–
Kathy Ross crafts letter shapes / Kathy Ross; illustrated by Jan Barger.
p. cm. — (Learning is fun!)
ISBN 0-7613-2103-9 (lib. bdg.) ISBN 0-7613-1490-3 (pbk.)
Handicraft—Juvenile literature. 2. Alphabet—Juvenile literature. [1. Handicraft. 2. Alphabet.]
I. Barger, Jan, 1948- ill. II. Title. III. Learning is fun! (Brookfield, Conn.)
TT160 .R7142337 2002
745.5—dc21 [[E]] 2001030132

Published by
The Millbrook Press, Inc.
2 Old New Milford Road
Brookfield, Connecticut 06804
www.millbrookpress.com

Printed in the United States of America
(lib)   5 4 3 2 1
(pbk)   5 4 3 2 1

Table of Contents

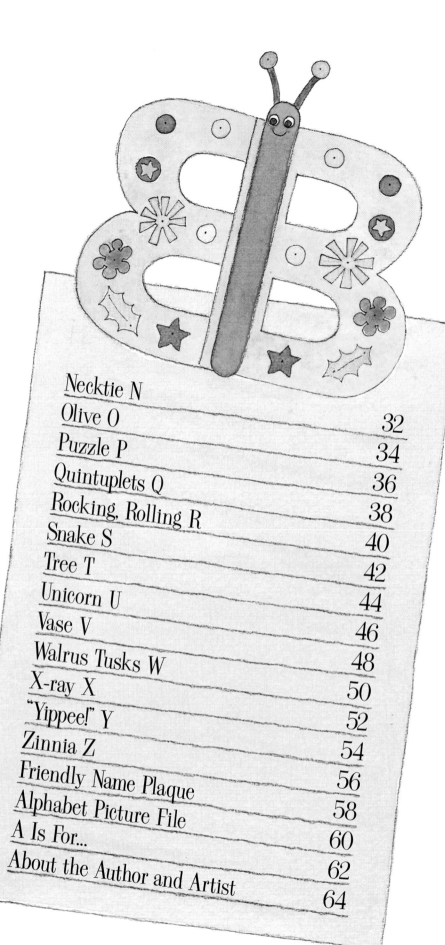

Introduction for Parents or Teachers

Each of the crafts in this book has been made with a standard block-type capital letter. To make each craft, you can trace the letter shape that is provided in this book for each letter of the alphabet. Printing letters from a clear, bold typeface on the computer at 72 points and then enlarging on a copy machine will also work.

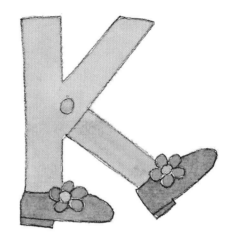

The best choice for making lots of letters quickly and easily for a group would be to use a die-cutting machine with a set of alphabet dies such as those made by Ellison or Accucut. Using a cutting machine will make these fun and easy projects an excellent learning activity choice for an entire class. Because the letter dies come in many different sizes, I have left the size of the letter to be used up to you. Each of these projects will be successful when done in proportion to the size of the letter being used.

Creatively involving children in projects that associate the letter shape with the letter sound makes learning about the alphabet fun.

Kathy Ross

A

Turn the letter A into an airplane.

Here is what you need:

construction paper letter A   sticker stars   paper clip

Here is what you do:

1. Fold the letter A in half.

2. Fold the two bottom legs of the A down at a right angle to make wings for the airplane.

3. Decorate the A airplane with sticker stars.

4. Slide a small paper clip over the nose of the plane to give it weight.

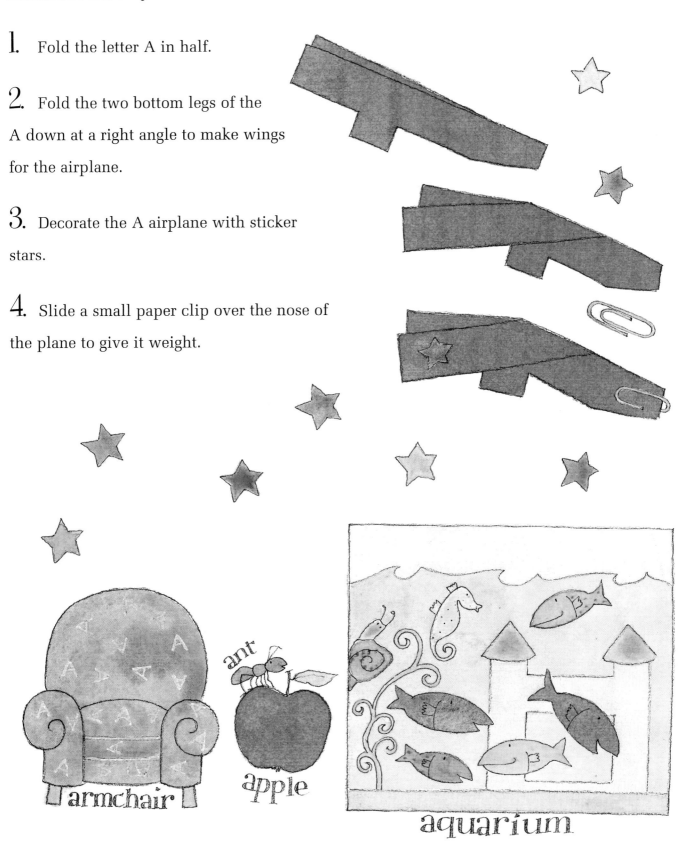

armchair

ant
apple

aquarium

Go land the letter A airplane on A objects around the house.

B

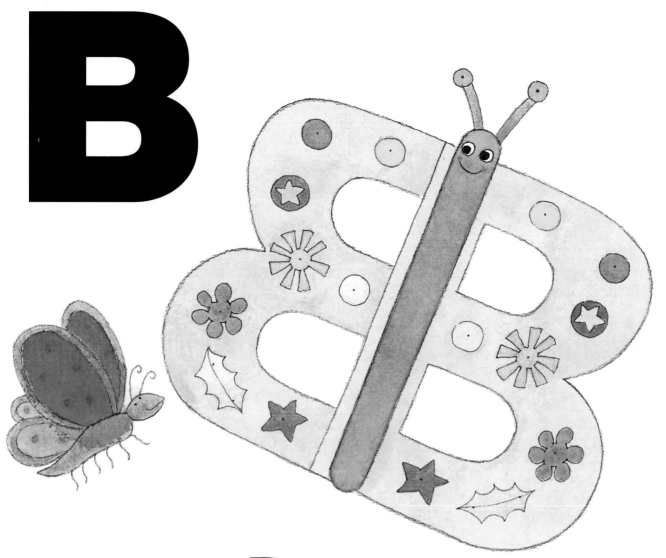

Turn two letter Bs into a pretty butterfly.

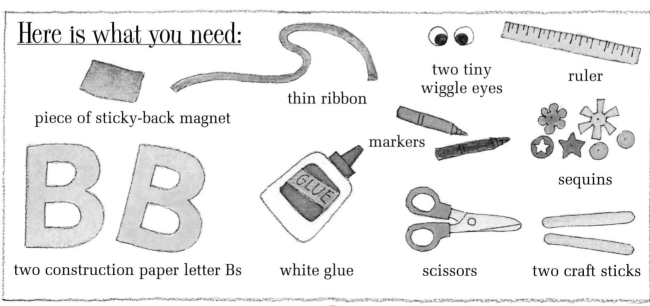

Here is what you need:

thin ribbon

two tiny wiggle eyes

ruler

piece of sticky-back magnet

markers

sequins

two construction paper letter Bs

white glue

scissors

two craft sticks

Here is what you do:

1. Use the markers to color one side of each craft stick.

2. Glue the straight side of each letter B on the uncolored side of one of the craft sticks, so that the two Bs stick out on each side to form the wings of the butterfly.

3. Glue the second craft stick, color side up, over the first stick to form the body of the butterfly.

4. Glue two tiny wiggle eyes to the top portion of the stick.

5. Draw a mouth with a marker.

6. Cut two 2-inch (5-cm) pieces of thin ribbon for the antennae. Glue the antennae sticking up from the back of the top of the head. Glue a round sequin to the tip of each antenna.

7. Decorate the wings of the B butterfly with sequins.

8. Add a piece of sticky-back magnet to the back of the butterfly.

Cut pictures of things starting with the letter B from magazines and glue them on a sheet of paper. The B butterfly can hold the pictures on the refrigerator for you.

C

Use lots of letter **C**s to make a **caterpillar**.

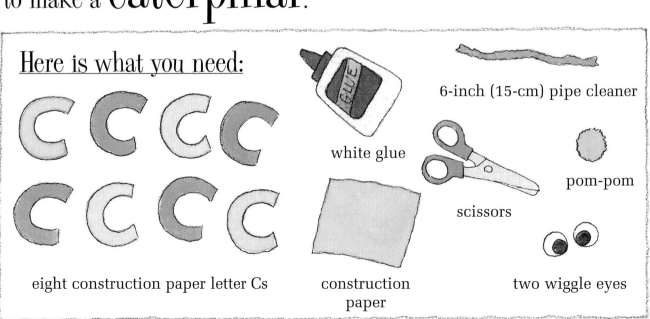

Here is what you need:

white glue

6-inch (15-cm) pipe cleaner

scissors

pom-pom

eight construction paper letter Cs

construction paper

two wiggle eyes

Here is what you do:

1. Glue the eight Cs together in a row to create the body of the caterpillar.

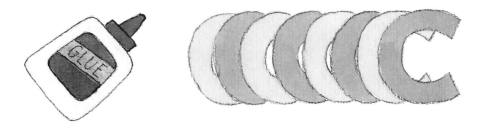

2. To make the head, cut a round circle about the same size as the Cs from the construction paper. Bend the pipe cleaner in half and tip the ends to make antennae for the caterpillar. Glue the antennae sticking up from the head.

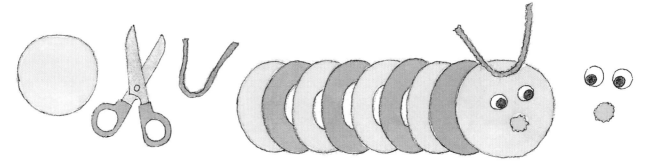

3. Glue the two wiggle eyes and the pom-pom nose on the head to give the caterpillar a face.

Crawl around with your letter C caterpillar looking for things that begin with the letter C.

D

Use two letter Ds to make the bill for this duck mask.

Here is what you need:

crayon

9-inch (23-cm) paper plate

white glue

craft feathers

ruler

two construction
paper letter Ds

yarn

scissors

hole punch

Here is what you do:

1. Hold the eating side of the plate to your face and use the crayon to mark where the eyeholes should be on the mask.

2. Cut the eyeholes out.

3. Glue the straight side of the two letter Ds together. Fold the rounded part of the Ds out in opposite directions to make the beak for the duck. Glue the beak to the mask below the eyeholes.

4. Glue some craft feathers sticking up from the top of the head.

5. Punch a hole in the middle of each side of the mask.

6. Cut two 2-foot (61-cm) lengths of yarn. Tie the end of each piece of yarn through each hole to make ties for the mask.

Put on the letter D duck mask and do things that start with the letter D. You could dance, dip down, duck, or draw. What other D things could you do?

13

E

Turn the letter E into an elephant.

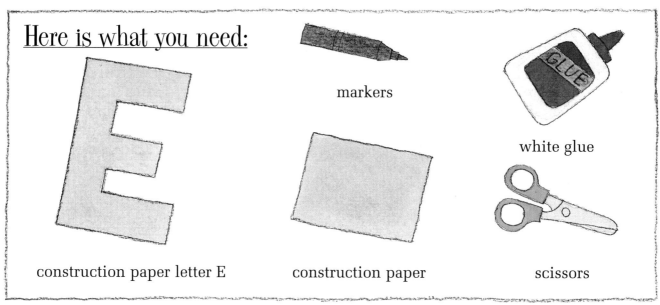

Here is what you need:

markers

white glue

construction paper letter E

construction paper

scissors

Here is what you do:

1. Fold a piece of construction paper in half and cut an elephant ear shape on the fold. Unfold the ears.

2. Turn the letter E so that the straight part is on top. Glue the ears to the top center of the E so that the middle bar of the E hangs down to form the trunk of the elephant.

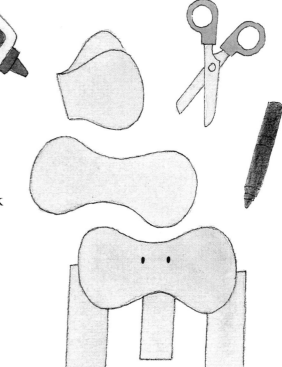

3. Use the marker to give the elephant eyes.

How about making eleven letter E elephants? Glue them on a sheet of construction paper and you'll have a herd of E elephants.

F

Turn the letter **F** into a **flower**.

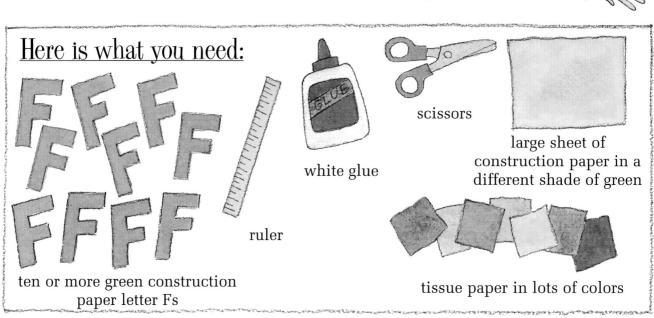

Here is what you need:

ten or more green construction paper letter Fs

ruler

white glue

scissors

large sheet of construction paper in a different shade of green

tissue paper in lots of colors

Here is what you do:

1. For each flower cut three 3-inch (8-cm) circles of tissue paper from three different shades of the same color. Stack the tissue circles together.

2. To make the flower head, pinch the tissue circles together at the center and make a tiny twist in the tissue to hold the shape.

3. Glue the flower head to the end of the top of a letter F. Round off the top corner of the F to make it look like a bent flower stem.

4. Glue lots of flowers in different colors onto the sheet of green construction paper.

Now you'll have a whole **field** of letter F flowers!

G

KEEP OUT!

Turn the letter G into a floating ghost in a box.

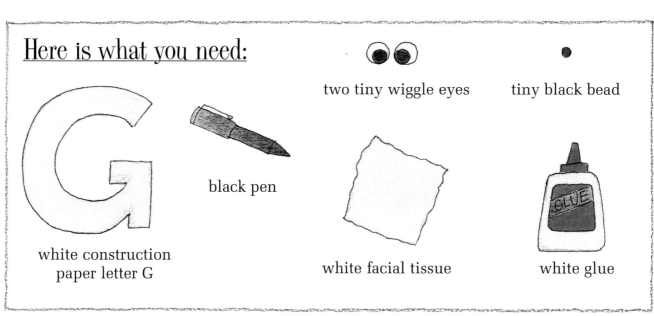

Here is what you need:

two tiny wiggle eyes

tiny black bead

black pen

white construction
paper letter G

white facial tissue

white glue

18

Here is what you do:

1. Turn the letter G on the open side. Use the pen to draw a line across the bottom to make it look like a box with an open lid. Write a warning on the box.

2. Cover the curved part of the G with glue. Fold the tissue around the curved part of the G to make the ghost.

3. Glue the two wiggle eyes and the bead on the top of the ghost to make a face.

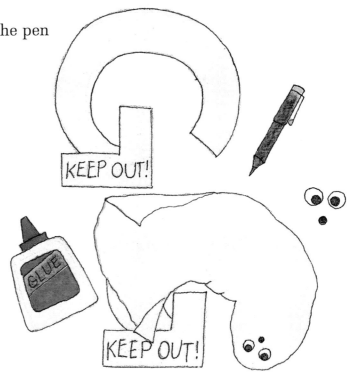

The letter G ghost is hungry. Can you find some magazine pictures of foods that begin with the letter G? (This ghost will only gobble G foods!)

Turn the letter **H** into a horse.

Here is what you need:

construction paper
letter H

yarn

markers

scissors

white glue

construction paper scraps

Here is what you do:

1. Fold the letter H in half, top to bottom, to form the body of the horse.

2. Cut a neck and head for the horse from construction paper scraps.

3. Use the markers to give the horse a face, a mane, and an ear on each side.

4. Glue the head into the fold at one end of the body.

5. Cut some strands of yarn for the tail of the horse. Unravel the yarn strands. Glue one end of the strands into the fold at the back of the horse.

6. Cut a saddle for the horse from a folded piece of construction paper. Glue the saddle on the back of the horse.

To make a home for the letter H horse, turn a box over and cut a door in one side. Paint the outside of the box, and decorate the inside with pictures of things that start with the letter H.

21

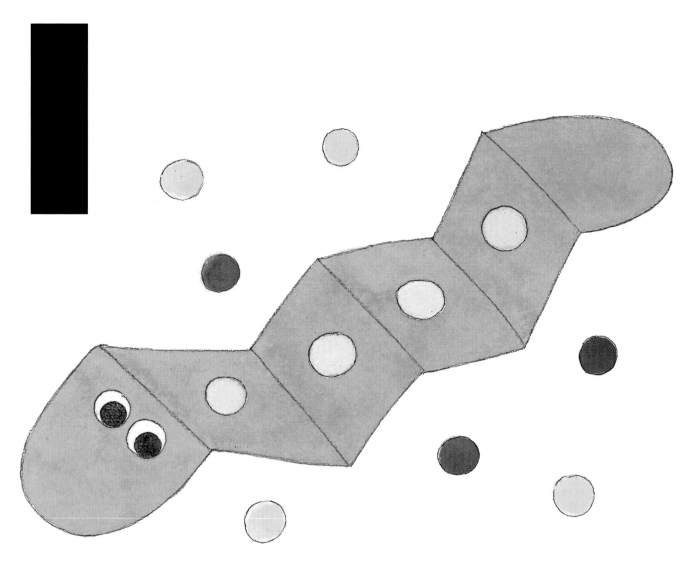

Turn the letter I into an **inchworm**.

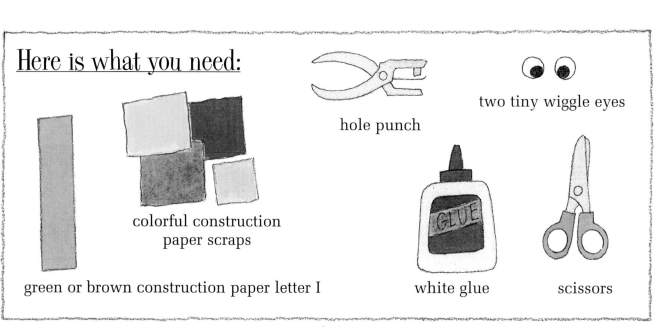

Here is what you need:

hole punch

two tiny wiggle eyes

colorful construction paper scraps

green or brown construction paper letter I

white glue

scissors

Here is what you do:

1. Round off the corners at both ends of the letter I to make the inchworm.

2. Fold the inchworm back and forth like you would to make a fan.

3. Glue the two wiggle eyes to one end of the inchworm.

4. Punch some dots out of the colorful construction paper. Glue the punched-out dots on the body of the inchworm for spots.

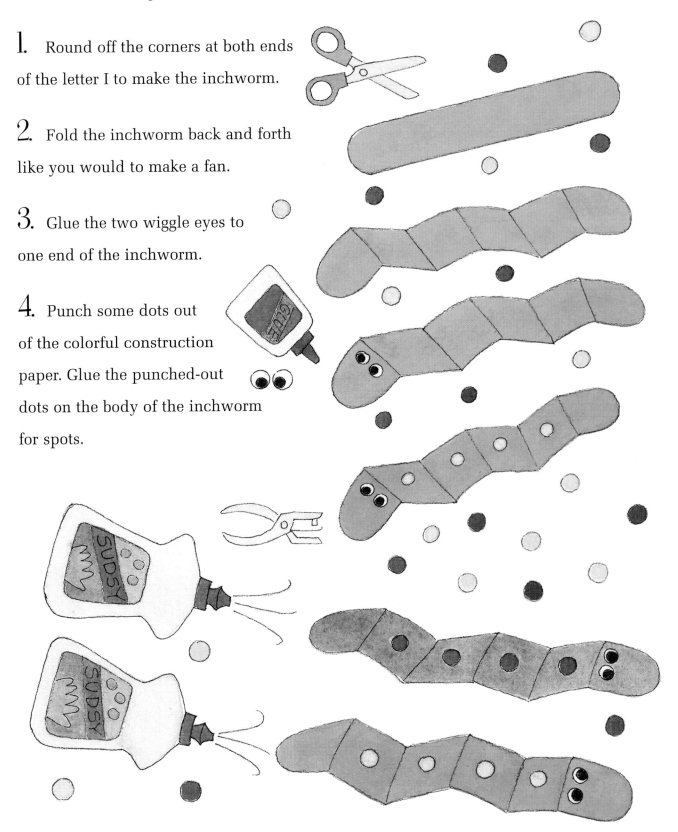

Make two letter I inchworms and have a race with a friend. Squeeze air from empty detergent bottles to propel the inchworms across the floor.

23

J

Turn two letter Js into a **jolly juggler**.

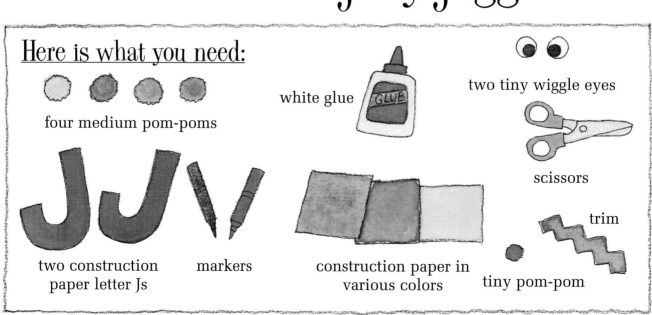

Here is what you need:

four medium pom-poms

white glue

two tiny wiggle eyes

scissors

two construction paper letter Js

markers

construction paper in various colors

trim

tiny pom-pom

24

Here is what you do:

1. Glue the two Js onto a piece of construction paper, with the side of one J over the side of the other and the hooks sticking out on each side to look like arms.

2. Cut a circle head from construction paper. Glue the head over the top portion of the center of the two Js.

3. Cut a triangle-shaped hat from construction paper. Glue the hat on the top part of the head.

4. Glue the wiggle eyes below the hat. Use the markers to draw a nose and mouth.

5. Glue the tiny pom-pom to the tip of the hat. Decorate the hat by gluing on the trim.

6. Glue a medium pom-pom to the top of each hook arm of the J and two more up in the air.

Can you think of some other actions that start with the letter J that the letter J juggler might do? How about jump or jiggle? Can you do that, too?

K

Make a letter K that **kicks.**

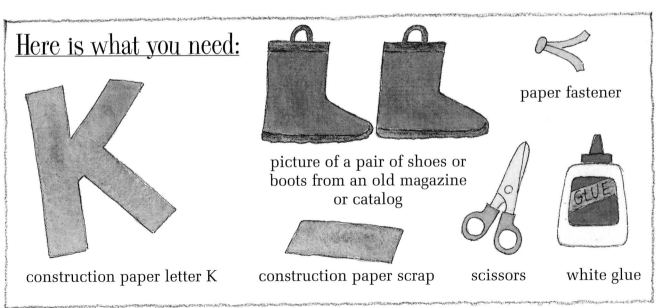

Here is what you need:

construction paper letter K

picture of a pair of shoes or boots from an old magazine or catalog

paper fastener

construction paper scrap

scissors

white glue

Here is what you do:

1. Cut the bottom leg off the letter K. Cut a strip of construction paper to glue to the top of the cut leg to extend it behind the middle of the rest of the letter K. Glue the extension strip on the cut piece.

2. Reattach the leg to the K with a paper fastener so that the leg swings back and forth to kick.

3. Cut out a pair of boots or shoes from an old catalog or magazine to fit the bottom of the letter K.

4. Glue a shoe or boot to each leg of the letter K.

Go through an old magazine looking for pictures of things that start with the letter K. Whenever you spot one, have the letter K kick it.

L

Make a **lizard** from the letter **L**.

Here is what you need:

red yarn

white glue

two tiny wiggle eyes

piece of sticky-back magnet

rickrack trim

green construction
paper letter L

scissors

masking tape

green pipe cleaner

Here is what you do:

1. Round off the edge of the top of the letter L for the head of the lizard. Also round off the bottom corner.

2. Cut the bottom end of the letter L into a point for the tail of the lizard.

3. Cut two pieces of pipe cleaner to stick out on each side of the front and the back of the lizard for the legs. Glue the legs on the back of the letter L. Secure the glued legs by covering them with a strip of masking tape to hold them in place while the glue dries.

4. Cut a piece of red yarn for the tongue of the lizard. Glue one end of the yarn under the head end of the letter L.

5. Glue the two wiggle eyes on the head.

6. Decorate the body of the lizard with a strip of rickrack.

7. Put a piece of sticky-back magnet on the back of the letter L lizard.

This letter L lizard is perfect for holding lists on the refrigerator. Make some long narrow pieces of paper with lines across to use for lists.

29

M

Make a **mouse** with the letter M.

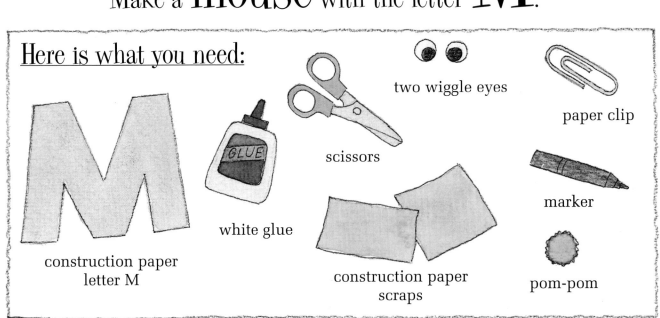

Here is what you need:

two wiggle eyes

paper clip

scissors

marker

white glue

construction paper
letter M

construction paper
scraps

pom-pom

Here is what you do:

1. Use the marker to draw tiny claws on the two outer bars of the letter M, which will become the front legs of the mouse. Pull the two outer bars of the letter M behind the center and glue them together. Use a paper clip to hold them together while the glue is drying.

2. Glue a pom-pom nose to the point of the letter M. Glue the two wiggle eyes above the nose.

3. Cut two round ears from the construction paper. Glue an ear to the top of the letter M on each side.

Can you name some munchies that the letter M mouse might eat that start with the letter M?

N

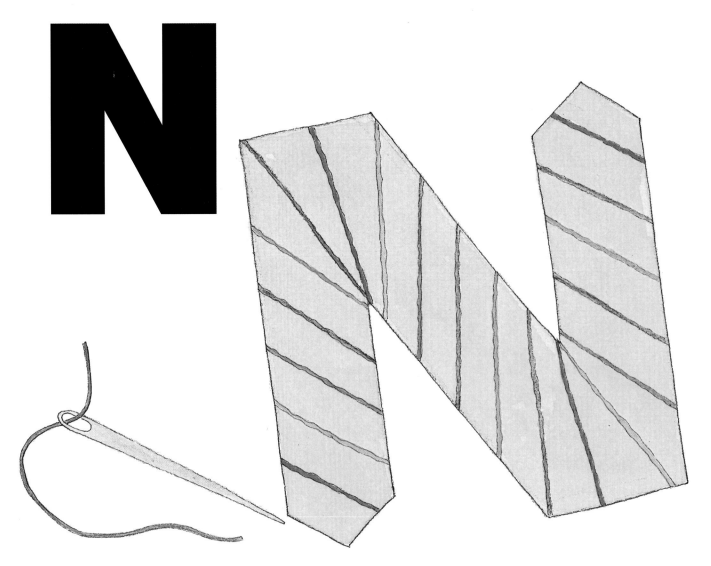

Turn the letter N into a necktie of your own design.

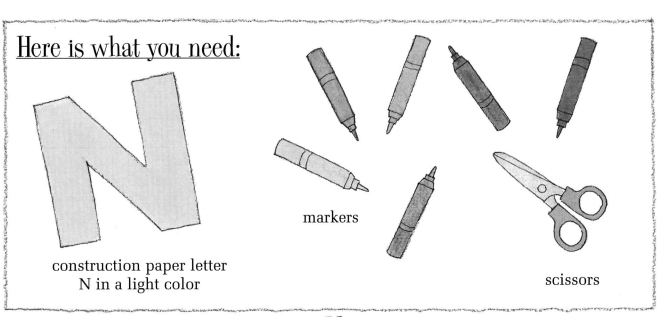

Here is what you need:

construction paper letter
N in a light color

markers

scissors

Here is what you do:

1. Trim the two ends of the letter N into points to resemble a necktie.

2. Use the markers to make a design on the necktie.

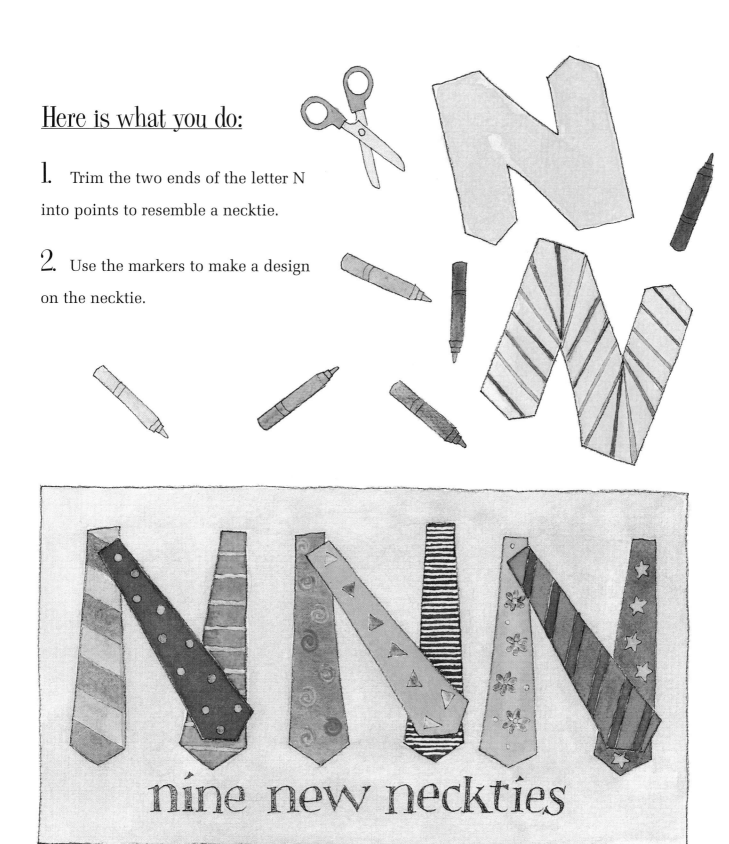

nine new neckties

Cut pictures of **neckties** from old catalogs. On a sheet of construction paper, glue each set of three together in the shape of the letter N.

O

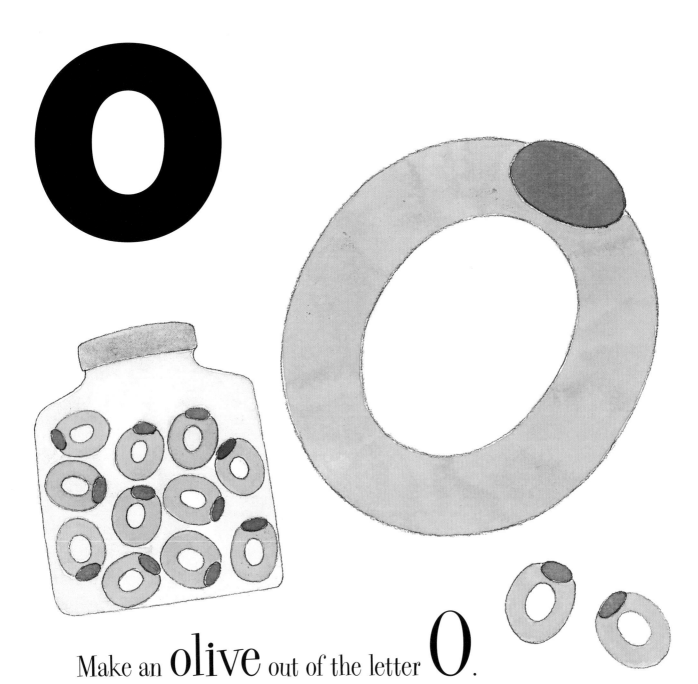

Make an **olive** out of the letter O.

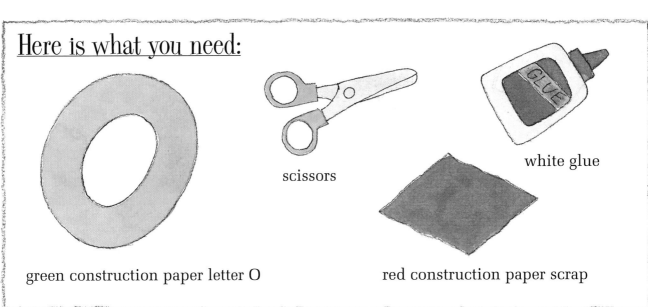

Here is what you need:

green construction paper letter O

scissors

white glue

red construction paper scrap

34

Here is what you do:

1. Cut a small, round oval from the red construction paper to make the pimento stuffed in the top of a green olive.

2. Glue the red pimento across the top of the letter O.

ostrich

owl

octopus

Make a collage of letter O olives glued on orange paper.

P

Make a **puzzle** with the letter P.

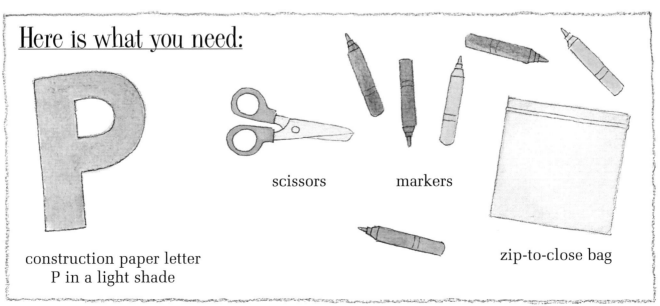

Here is what you need:

construction paper letter
P in a light shade

scissors

markers

zip-to-close bag

Here is what you do:

1. Use the markers to decorate the letter P.

2. Cut the letter P into pieces to make a puzzle.

3. Try putting the P puzzle back together. Store it in the zip-to-close bag.

4. To make it more challenging, make more than one letter P puzzle and mix all the pieces together.

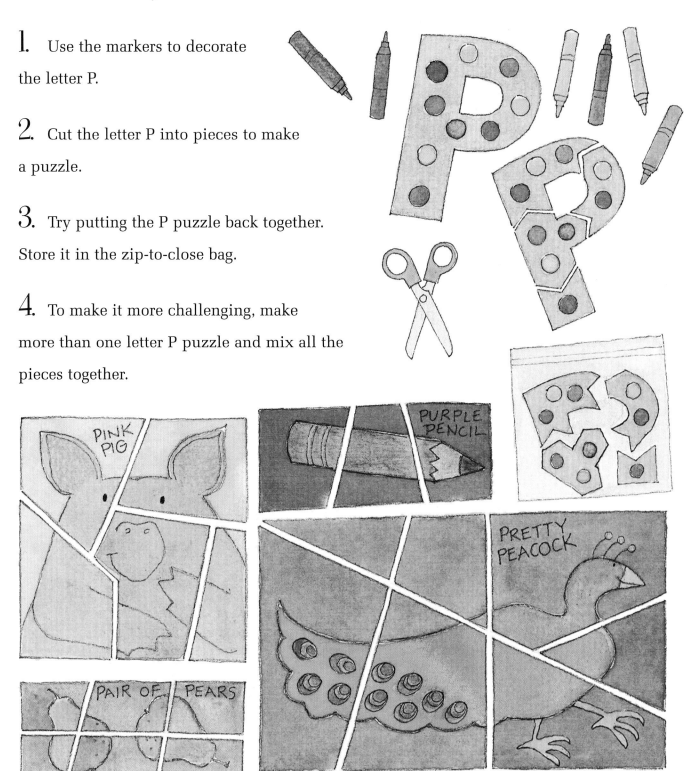

PINK PIG

PURPLE PENCIL

PRETTY PEACOCK

PAIR OF PEARS

Find some magazine pictures of things that start with the letter P. Glue each picture to cereal box cardboard. When the glue has dried, cut the pictures apart to make P word picture puzzles. Store each puzzle in a zip-to-close bag.

Q

Make a set of quintuplets with five letter Qs.

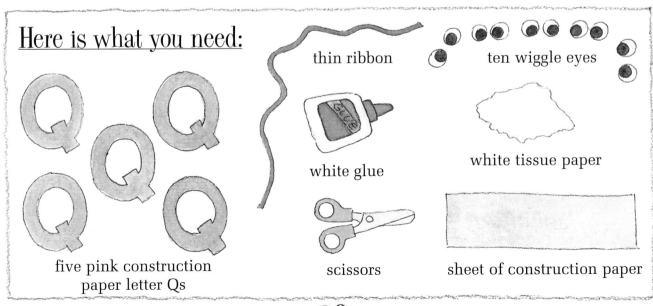

Here is what you need:

thin ribbon

ten wiggle eyes

white glue

white tissue paper

five pink construction paper letter Qs

scissors

sheet of construction paper

Here is what you do:

1. Glue the five letter Qs in a row across a strip of construction paper.

2. Glue two wiggle eyes in the center of each Q.

3. Make five bows from the thin ribbon. Glue a bow across the tail of each Q for the tie on each baby bonnet.

4. Cut five strips of tissue paper. Rub glue around each Q. Gather strips of tissue around each Q to look like the ruffle of a baby bonnet.

Make a **quilt** to hang below the letter Q **quintuplets** by covering a sheet of construction paper with squares cut from old catalogs and magazines.

R

Make a **rocking, rolling, red** letter R.

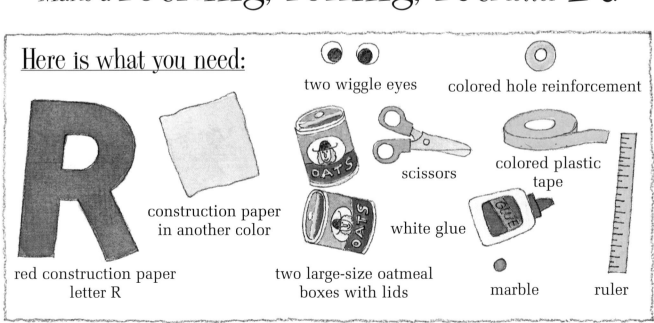

Here is what you need:

two wiggle eyes

colored hole reinforcement

red construction paper
letter R

construction paper
in another color

two large-size oatmeal
boxes with lids

scissors

white glue

colored plastic
tape

marble

ruler

Here is what you do:

1. Cut a 1 ½-inch (4-cm) rim from the top of one oatmeal box. Snap the lid on the rim. Discard the bottom portion of the box.

2. Remove the lid from the second oatmeal box. Drop the marble in the cut container, then glue on the second lid over the opening.

3. Glue a circle of construction paper onto both sides.

4. Cover the sides of the container with the colored tape.

5. Glue the letter R on one of the lids. Glue on the wiggle eyes and the hole reinforcement to give the letter R a surprised-looking face.

6. Stand the container on edge and give it a push to make the letter R rock and roll.

Make two **rocking, rolling** letter Rs and have a **race** with a friend.

41

S

Turn the letter S into a **snake**.

Here is what you need:

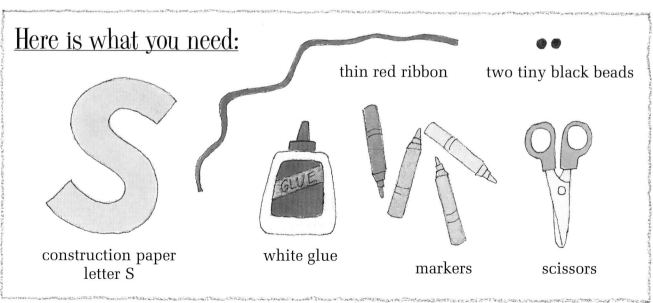

thin red ribbon

two tiny black beads

construction paper
letter S

white glue

markers

scissors

Here is what you do:

1. Round off all corners on the letter S. Cut a tongue for the snake from the red ribbon. Cut a triangle shape out of one end of the ribbon to make a forked tongue. Glue the flat end of the tongue under the top end of the letter S.

2. Glue the two beads on the letter S above the tongue for the eyes.

Use the markers to draw a design on the body of the snake.

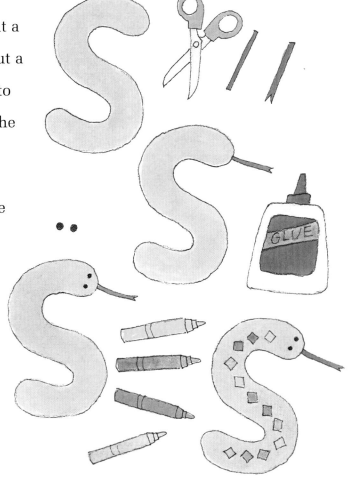

Make a small paper accordion-style booklet by folding a strip of adding machine tape or construction paper back and forth as if you were making a fan. Glue a magazine picture of something that starts with S on each page of the book. Punch a hole in the outer corner of each page. Wiggle a pipe cleaner snake through the pages of the book, naming each S word as the snake wiggles by it.

T

Turn the letter T into a **tree**.

Here is what you need:

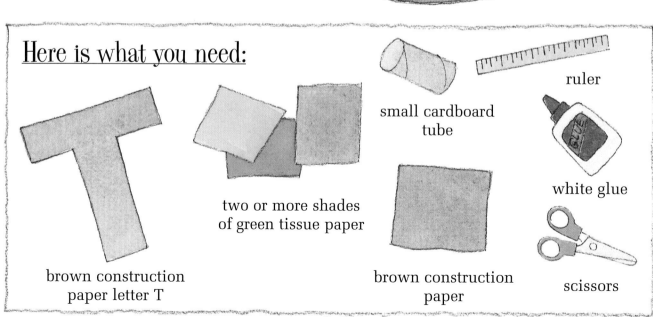

brown construction
paper letter T

two or more shades
of green tissue paper

small cardboard
tube

ruler

white glue

brown construction
paper

scissors

Here is what you do:

1. Cover the tube with brown construction paper.

2. Glue the letter T to the side of the tube to look like the trunk and branches of a tree.

3. Rub glue around the top inside of the tube.

4. Cut three 8-inch (20-cm) squares of tissue paper. Stack them at different angles and tuck the center of the tissue stack into the top of the tube to form the top of the tree.

5. Use the scissors to "prune" the treetop.

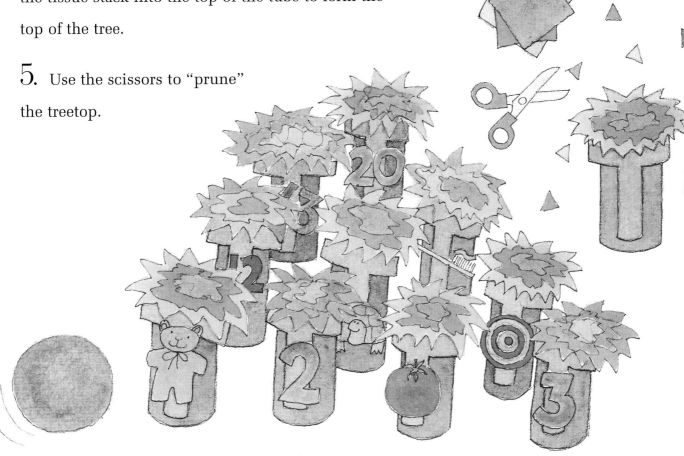

Make a forest of ten letter T trees. Glue a magazine picture of a T word to the trunk of each tree. Set up the trees like tenpins (bowling pins). Try to knock them down with a foam or rubber ball. Name all the T words you knock down.

U

Make a **unicorn** from the letter U.

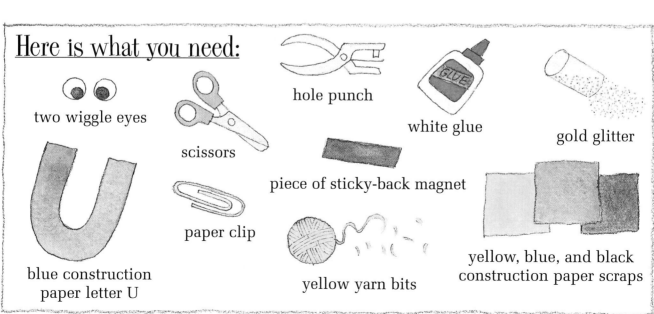

Here is what you need:

two wiggle eyes

scissors

hole punch

white glue

gold glitter

blue construction paper letter U

paper clip

piece of sticky-back magnet

yellow yarn bits

yellow, blue, and black construction paper scraps

Here is what you do:

1. Pull the two ends of the letter U together and glue them. Use a paper clip to hold the two ends in place while the glue dries. This will be the head of the unicorn.

2. Cut two ears for the unicorn from blue paper. Glue an ear sticking out from each side of the top of the head.

3. Cut a horn for the unicorn from yellow paper. Cover the horn with glue and sprinkle it with gold glitter. Glue the horn to the top of the head between the two ears.

4. Glue the yellow yarn bits over the base of the horn to make the forelock of the unicorn.

5. Glue the two wiggle eyes on the two sides of the letter U below the forelock.

6. Punch out two dots from the black paper for nostrils. Glue the nostrils on the bottom part of the letter U.

7. Attach a piece of sticky-back magnet to the back of the unicorn head.

Find magazine pictures of things that start with the letter U for the letter U unicorn to hold on the refrigerator.

V

Turn the letter V into a **vase** of pretty flowers.

Here is what you need:

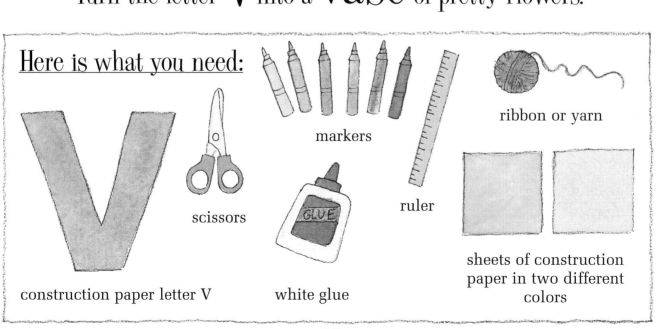

construction paper letter V

scissors

markers

white glue

ruler

ribbon or yarn

sheets of construction paper in two different colors

Here is what you do:

1. Trim about 1 inch (2.5 cm) off each end of the four sides of one of the sheets of paper. Glue the letter V to the bottom part of the paper to look like a vase.

2. Use the markers to draw a vase full of flowers.

3. Cut a 12-inch (30-cm)-long piece of ribbon or yarn.

4. Glue the paper to the other, larger sheet of paper to make a frame, first slipping the two ends of the yarn between the two sheets of paper at the top to make a hanger.

vulture

violin

violet

Make another letter V vase picture, but instead of drawing flowers at the ends of the stems glue on magazine pictures of things that start with the letter V.

49

W

Use the letter **W** to make the tusks of a **walrus**.

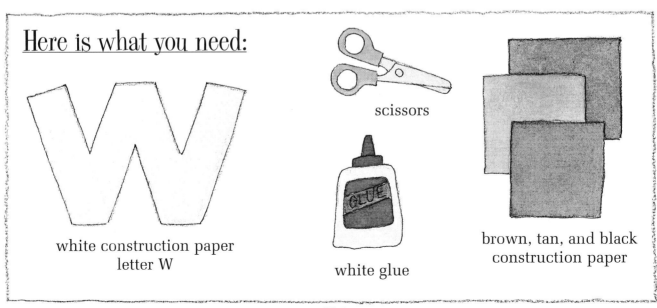

Here is what you need:

white construction paper
letter W

scissors

white glue

brown, tan, and black
construction paper

Here is what you do:

1. Cut a circle from the brown paper for the head of the walrus.

2. Cut an oval shape about as wide as the circle from the tan paper. Cut two bumps on one side of the oval like the top of a heart. Glue the tan paper, bump side down, to the bottom of the brown circle head to make the jowls for the walrus.

3. Glue the top of the letter W behind the bottom of the jowls so that it looks like two tusks hanging down.

4. Cut three small black circles. Glue two on the head for the eyes, and glue one on the top center of the jowls for the nose.

Cut lots of blue construction paper letter Ws. Glue them to a sheet of blue paper to look like waves of water. Glue the head of the letter W walrus on the paper to look like it is sticking up out of the water. Cut an ice floe from white construction paper. Glue the ice floe in the water. Find some magazine pictures of things that begin with the letter W to glue on the ice floe.

X

Make an X ray of the letter X.

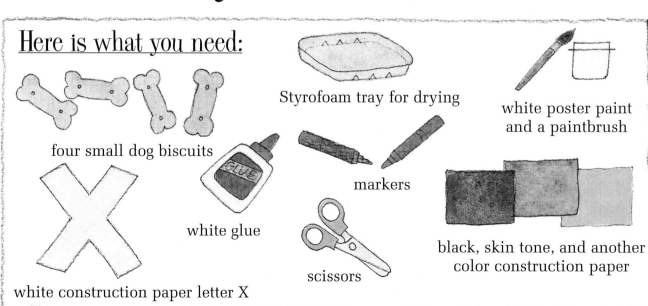

Here is what you need:

four small dog biscuits

Styrofoam tray for drying

white poster paint and a paintbrush

white construction paper letter X

white glue

markers

scissors

black, skin tone, and another color construction paper

Here is what you do:

1. Paint the four dog biscuits white and let them dry on the Styrofoam tray.

2. Cut a square of black paper slightly bigger than the paper X to be the X-ray machine.

3. Glue the X to the black paper square.

4. Cut a head and hands from the skin tone paper. Use the markers to give the head a face and hair.

5. Glue the bottom edge of the head behind the top of the black square of paper. Glue a hand sticking up on each side of the letter X.

6. Cut shoes from construction paper. Glue a shoe sticking out below the black paper from each side of the bottom of the letter X.

7. Glue a white "bone" on each part of the letter X.

X means a kiss. Make a card for your favorite grown-up and write lots of letter Xs inside.

Y

Turn two letter Ys into you yelling, "Yippee!"

Here is what you need:

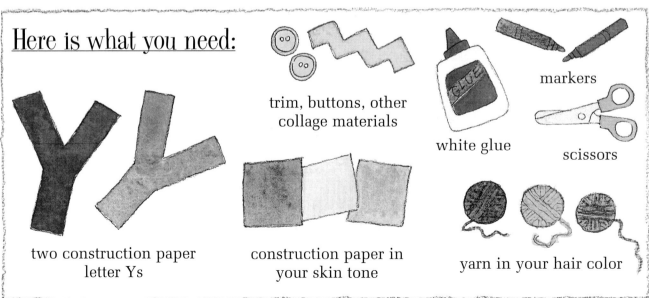

two construction paper
letter Ys

construction paper in
your skin tone

trim, buttons, other
collage materials

white glue

markers

scissors

yarn in your hair color

54

Here is what you do:

1. Glue the stems of the two letter Ys together with the forked part of each letter going in the opposite direction. This will be the body of the figure.

2. Cut a head, hands, and feet from the construction paper.

3. Glue hands on the ends of the top of one letter Y and the feet at the ends of the top of the other letter Y.

4. Draw a face on the head with the markers. Glue on some yarn bits for hair. Glue the head to the Y that has the hands glued to it.

5. Decorate the clothes using the collage materials.

Make a bunch of different letter Y people, and find or draw a picture of something that starts with the letter Y for each Y person to hold up.

Z

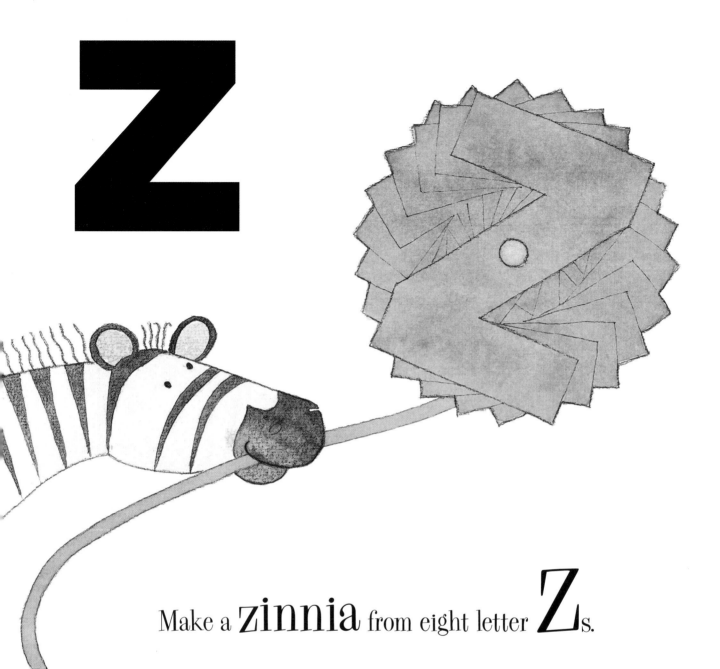

Make a *zinnia* from eight letter **Z**s.

Here is what you need:

eight construction paper
letter Zs in the same
bright color

scissors

pencil

white glue

paper
fastener

masking tape

thin green ribbon

small hole punch

piece of sticky-back
magnet

Here is what you do:

1. Stack the eight letter Zs. Punch a small hole through the middle of all eight letter Zs. You may need to do this in two piles of four Zs. Use a pencil to mark where to punch the hole in the second stack so that the Zs line up.

2. Holding the letter Zs in a stack, attach them together by putting the paper fastener through the holes and bending out the ends in the back.

3. Fan out the Zs around the fastener until they form a complete circle, the Z zinnia.

4. Cut a 12-inch (30-cm) length of green ribbon. Glue one end of the ribbon to the back of the flower so that it hangs down to form a stem. Cover the glued end with a piece of masking tape to secure it while the glue dries.

5. Attach a piece of sticky-back magnet to the back of the zinnia and stick it on the refrigerator.

Make zillions of letter Z zinnias in different colors to decorate the refrigerator.

Friendly Name Plaque

Turn the letters of your name into
a name plaque for your bedroom door.

Here is what you need:

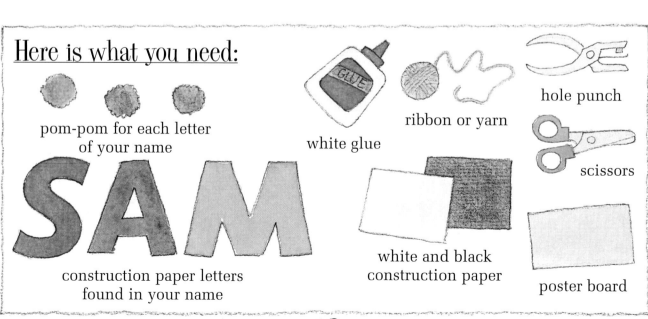

pom-pom for each letter
of your name

white glue

ribbon or yarn

hole punch

scissors

construction paper letters
found in your name

white and black
construction paper

poster board

Here is what you do:

1. Cut a rectangle of poster board just long enough to fit the letters of your name.

2. Glue the letters of your name on the poster board.

3. Cut white eyes and black pupils for each letter from the construction paper.

4. Glue a pair of eyes on each letter. Move the location of the pupils around on each pair of eyes to make them look funny.

5. Glue a pom-pom nose on each letter.

6. Punch a hole in the top of the poster board at each end.

7. Cut a length of ribbon or yarn to thread through the two holes. Tie the ends together to make a hanger.

You can use additional collage materials to personalize the letters of your name. You could cut hats or shoes from magazines or add bows or buttons. Have fun making your name plaque as individual as you are.

Alphabet Picture File

Make an envelope file for saving pictures of things that start with each letter of the alphabet.

Here is what you need:

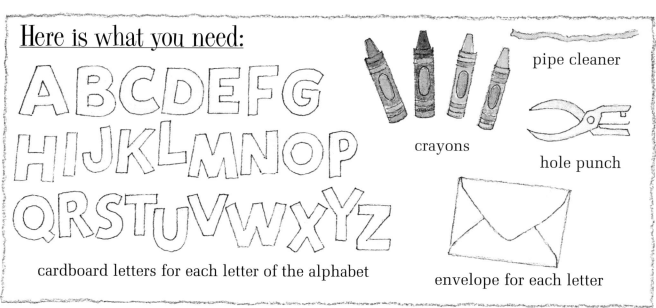

A B C D E F G
H I J K L M N O P
Q R S T U V W X Y Z

cardboard letters for each letter of the alphabet

pipe cleaner

crayons

hole punch

envelope for each letter

Here is what you do:

1. For each envelope file, put the cardboard letter inside the envelope. Rub over the cardboard letter on the outside of the envelope with the side of a crayon to make the letter appear on the outside of the envelope. This is called a "rubbing" and is fun to do.

2. Punch a hole in the top of the envelope.

3. Thread a 6-inch (15-cm) pipe cleaner through the hole and wrap the ends together to form a circle. Each time you make a different letter envelope you can add it to the pipe-cleaner ring.

4. Use the envelopes to keep pictures of things beginning with each letter of the alphabet in good order.

The cardboard letters can be used over and over to make rubbings on sheets of paper. They are also fun to trace around on paper.

A Is For...

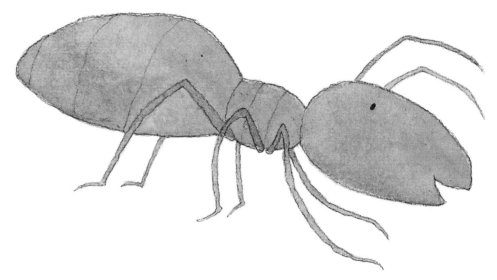

Decorate a paper letter of each letter of the alphabet
with something that starts with that letter.

Here is an idea for each letter:

A apple seeds   B buttons   C cotton balls   D dots
(punch them with
a hole punch)   E eggshells

F feathers   G glitter   H holes (punch some   I ink stamps
out of the letter with a   (print on the letter)
hole punch)

J jewels (craft jewels or paper ones cut from magazines and catalogs)

K keys

L lace

M macaroni

N newspaper

O oatmeal

P popcorn kernels

Q quarter rubbings (cut out rubbings to glue on letter)

R ribbon

S sequins

T tissue paper

U upside-down pictures (cut from magazines)

V velvet (use velvet ribbon strips)

W wallpaper

X Xs (draw Xs on the letter)

Y yarn

Z zigzag (use rickrack for a zigzag pattern)

Glue each letter to a page and make a letter collage book. I bet you'll have lots of other ideas for decorating each letter.

About the Author and Artist

Twenty-five years as a teacher and director of nursery school programs have given **Kathy Ross** extensive experience in guiding young children through craft projects. Among the more than forty craft books she has written are CRAFTS FOR ALL SEASONS, MAKE YOURSELF A MONSTER, THE BEST BIRTHDAY PARTIES EVER, CHRISTMAS ORNAMENTS KIDS CAN MAKE, and CRAFTS FROM YOUR FAVORITE CHILDREN'S SONGS. She is also the author of the popular *Holiday Crafts for Kids* series, and the *Crafts for Kids Who Are Wild About . . .* series.

Learn more about Kathy and download new crafts by visiting kathyross.com

Jan Barger, originally from Little Rock, Arkansas, now lives in Plumpton, East Sussex, with her husband and their cocker spaniel, Tosca. As well as writing and illustrating children's books, she designs greeting cards, sings with the Brighton Festival Chorus, and plays piccolo with the Sinfonia of Arun.